Animals on the Coast

LEVEL 9

DECODABLES BY jump!

Teaching Tips

Gold Level 9

This book focuses on developing reading independence, fluency, and comprehension.

Before Reading

- Ask readers what they think the book will be about based on the title. Have them support their answer.

Read the Book

- Encourage readers to read silently on their own.
- As readers encounter unfamiliar words, ask them to look for context clues to see if they can figure out what the words mean. Encourage them to locate boldfaced words in the glossary and ask questions to clarify the meaning of new vocabulary.
- Allow readers time to absorb the text and think about each chapter.
- Ask readers to write down any questions they have about the book's content.

After Reading

- Ask readers to summarize the book.
- Encourage them to point out anything they did not understand and ask questions.
- Ask readers to review the questions on page 23. Have them go back through the book to find answers. Have them write their answers on a separate sheet of paper.

© 2024 Booklife Publishing
This edition is published by arrangement with Booklife Publishing.

North American adaptations © 2024 Jump!
5357 Penn Avenue South
Minneapolis, MN 55419
www.jumplibrary.com

Decodables by Jump! are published by Jump! Library.
All rights reserved. No part of this book may be reproduced in any form without written permission from the publisher.

Library of Congress Cataloging-in-Publication Data is available at www.loc.gov or upon request from the publisher.

ISBN: 979-8-88996-909-9 (hardcover)
ISBN: 979-8-88996-910-5 (paperback)
ISBN: 979-8-88996-911-2 (ebook)

Table of Contents

What Is the Coast?

The coast is the strip of land by an ocean or a sea. Coasts can have many different features, such as beaches, mudflats, caves, and cliffs.

White cliffs

Sandy beach

These different types of land mean that coasts make very good homes for lots of animals. Some animals, such as gannets, find their homes on the cliffs. Some sea creatures might get pushed onto the beach by the ocean's waves.

Gannet

What Is a Rock Pool?

A rock pool is made when the **tide** goes out and leaves water in gaps between rocks. Animals can be found in rock pools. Some creatures get trapped in rock pools. Other creatures live on the rocks around them.

Rock pools can be lots of fun, but they can also be dangerous and slippery. If you visit a rock pool, you also need to be careful not to harm the creatures that live there.

What Are Dunes?

Dunes are large piles of sand that can be found along the coast. They are very important to our coasts and the **wildlife** that live there. Dunes can be very big or small. They are always changing.

Dunes

Dunes are made when wind blows sand into a pile. This usually happens when the sand is blown behind something, such as another dune. Dunes have two sides. They are the slip face and the windward side.

Slip face

Windward side

Dune Critters

Sand dunes are home to lots of different critters. Some critters include clown beetles, robber flies, and dune wolf spiders. Dune wolf spiders are the same color as the sand, so they can be hard to spot.

Dune wolf spider

Starfish

Starfish can often be found in rock pools. There are about 2,000 different types of starfish. Starfish have tough armor to protect them from **predators**.

Most starfish have five arms, but some can have up to 40 arms!

Shellfish

Shellfish are creatures that live in hard shells. Lots of coastal creatures eat shellfish. Some people do too. Many different shellfish can be found on beaches, such as mussels, clams, and cockles.

Mussels

Clams

Cockles

Gulls

There are many gull **species**, but people often just call them all seagulls. Gulls can live on sea cliffs, sand dunes, and even in towns and cities. They eat lots of different foods, such as fish, insects, and seeds.

Crabs and Hermit Crabs

Crabs have a hard outer shell to protect them. They also have 10 legs, two of which have claws on them. Be careful if you hold a crab. Some crabs could pinch you!

Hermit crabs are one type of crab. Unlike most crabs, hermit crabs do not have their own shells. Instead, they borrow shells they find. As they grow, hermit crabs leave their shells to find bigger ones.

Sea Anemones

Sea anemones look like plants with **tentacles**, but they are animals! They often stick to rocks, so they can sometimes be spotted in rock pools. Sea anemones are **venomous**, so they can be very dangerous.

Mouth

Tentacles

Seals

Seals are marine **mammals**. They can be found in most waters around the world, but they prefer cold waters. They have a thick layer of fat called blubber that keeps them warm. Seals often live in large groups on rocks.

Wading Birds

Wading birds walk around in the water looking for food. They have long legs and long beaks. These beaks help them catch food. Some wading birds catch fish, while others eat shellfish.

Herons are a type of wading bird.

Shrimp

There are many different types of shrimp, and they all look very different. Some shrimp are very colorful, while others are see-through. They can also be very small and very fast, which makes them hard to see.

Jellyfish

Unlike most sea creatures, jellyfish do not actually swim. Instead, they rely on ocean **currents** to move them around. However, this means they can sometimes be left on the beach when the tide goes out.

There are many different types of jellyfish, such as moon jellyfish, compass jellyfish, and blue jellyfish. Never touch a jellyfish. Even small jellyfish can have a very painful sting.

Moon jellyfish

Compass jellyfish

Blue jellyfish

Index

How to Use an Index

An index helps us find information in a book. Each word has a set of page numbers. These page numbers are where you can find information about that word.

Page numbers

Example: balloons 5, <u>8–10</u>, 19

Important word

This means page 8, page 10, and all the pages in between. Here, it means pages 8, 9, and 10.

Questions

1. How do rock pools form?

2. How many types of starfish are there?

3. Why are some sea anemones dangerous?

4. Using the Table of Contents, can you find which page you can read about gulls?

5. Using the Index, can you find a page in the book about shells?

6. Using the Glossary, can you define what tentacles are?

Glossary

currents:
Water that moves in a specific direction, especially through other water that has less movement.

mammals:
Warm-blooded animals that have hair or fur and usually give birth to live babies. Female mammals produce milk to feed their young.

predators:
Animals that hunt other animals for food.

species:
One of the groups into which similar animals and plants are divided.

tentacles:
Flexible structures used for eating or grabbing that are often near the mouth or head of an animal.

tide:
A change in sea level where the ocean waves rise and fall on the shore.

venomous:
Poisonous.

wildlife:
Wild creatures such as birds, mammals, and fish.